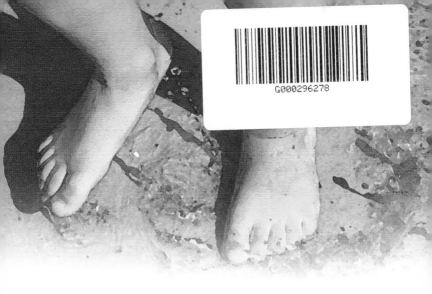

Those who accepted his message were baptized.
—Acts 2:41

Your baptism is a step of faith, an opportunity for you to confess your faith in the Lord Jesus Christ, witness to your associates, and experience the warmth of God's approval in a very meaningful way. I pray that this instructional material will be a blessing to your life.

—Jerry Brecheisen

What is *Baptism?*

*But when they believed Philip as he preached the good news
of the kingdom of God and the name of Jesus Christ,
they were baptized, both men and women.*
—Acts 8:12

Congratulations! You are taking a giant leap on your spiritual journey. Baptism is a way of publicly announcing your decision to commit your life to the Lord Jesus Christ and live by the instruction of His Word.

Baptism is not a shortcut to heaven. Paul reminds us: "For it is by grace you have been saved, through faith—and this not from yourselves, it is the gift of God—not by works, so that no one can boast" (Eph. 2:8–9). Ritual

BEGIN

alone offers you no eternal hope. Baptism does not ensure your acceptance by God and entrance into His kingdom any more than does standing in a puddle of water following a rainstorm.

Instead, baptism is outward, physical evidence of Christ's spiritual work deep within your heart. By submitting to baptism, you acknowledge your faith in His divine life and dynamic work of spiritual restoration and acceptance. You have repented of your sinful past, and Christ has given you a glorious future with present forgiveness and citizenship in His eternal kingdom.

- What does baptism mean to you?

- How is baptism a sacred and meaningful act?

- What other spiritual practices draw you closer to God and make you more like His Son?

NINGS

What Should I Do Before Baptism?

That is why you should examine yourself.
—I Corinthians II:28, NLT

Paul urged the Christians at Corinth to examine themselves before taking part in the sacrament of Communion. Likewise, you will want to prepare for your baptism as a believer.

The first step is to be sure you have been born again. Christians (Christ-ones) have two birthdays. Their chronological age is dated by the specific time and date of their arrival on planet Earth. Likewise, their spiritual age is determined by the specific moment in time when they trusted Christ as their Savior and pledged to serve Him as their Lord.

Have you experienced a specific moment when you "repented of sin" (were sorry enough for your sin to quit sinning) and personally asked

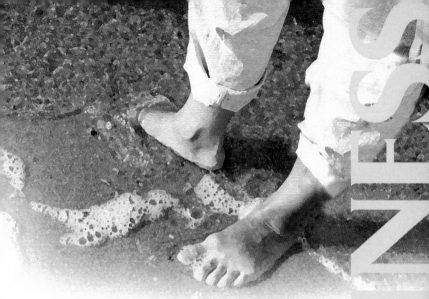

the Lord Jesus Christ into your heart and life? If not, it is
essential that you do so as an initial step in your life of faith.

The next step in your spiritual preparation is deciding to
make a public confession of your faith. God's army doesn't
need undercover agents.

Jesus said, "You are the light of the world. A city on a hill
cannot be hidden" (Matt. 5:14). Baptism is a conscious
decision to display your faith so brightly that it will be seen
clearly by every observer—whether one or one thousand.

- When did you trust Christ as your Savior?

- Do you have questions about what it means to be a
  Christian?

- Are you spiritually ready to be baptized?

How is This a Testimony to My New Faith?

If anyone acknowledges me publicly here on earth, I will openly acknowledge that person before my Father in heaven.
—Matthew 10:32, NLT

While in prison for preaching the gospel (good news about the life, death, and resurrection of the Lord Jesus Christ), Paul and Silas were given the opportunity to witness to the jailer who guarded them. When the jailer asked what he should do to be saved, "they replied, 'Believe in the Lord Jesus, and you will be saved—you and your household.' Then they spoke the word of the Lord to him and to all the others in his house. At that hour of the night the jailer took them and washed their wounds; then immediately he and all

CONFI

his family were baptized" (Acts 16:31-33). For the jailer, baptism was a tangible expression of his newfound faith.

In the same way, your baptism is a public declaration of independence from your past life and dependence upon Christ for your present and future life. The apostle Peter, in a letter of instruction and encouragement to persecuted New Testament Christians, wrote, "Praise be to the God and Father of our Lord Jesus Christ! In his great mercy he has given us new birth into a living hope through the resurrection of Jesus Christ from the dead" (1 Pet. 1:3).

Being baptized is like sending change of address cards to your loved ones and friends. You signify that the Savior has made you a brand-new spiritual citizen in a land without tears or time. So don't tiptoe into the baptismal waters. Take bold, triumphant steps—steps of declaration based upon the divine work of the Lord Jesus Christ.

- What does baptism say about your spiritual citizenship?

- Why should you take bold steps in your baptism?

- What will your baptism say to your family and friends?

The *Witness*
of *Baptism*

And you will be my witnesses.
—Acts 1:8

What are my options?" is a phrase often used in business and medical decisions. When it comes to witnessing, the only option is to do it! Jesus' last words to His disciples clearly formed a job description for their life's work: "You *will be* my witnesses." Though not every believer has the gift (divinely empowered ability) of evangelism, all believers are called to witness (tell others about the Lord's work in their life). *Not* witnessing is not an option. "'You are my witnesses,' declares the Lord" (Isa. 43:10).

The verbal response you give during the ritual of believer's baptism is a form of witnessing. You may have the opportunity to share how you

became a Christian or respond to your pastor's questions during the baptismal service. Even if you say nothing, your very participation in baptism is a witness to your family, to your friends, and to your associates.

Your baptism is a wonderful opportunity to share your faith in the Lord Jesus Christ. How can you make the most of this occasion? Start with a simple invitation. Your local church may even have printed invitations for you to send to family and friends.

Often it is most difficult to share our faith with our immediate family or close circle of friends. Inviting them to your baptism is a simple but effective way to follow the Lord's command.

- Whom do you know who has not yet heard the good news about Jesus?

- How do you feel about telling others about Christ?

- How will you include family and friends in your baptismal service?

Where Will I Be Baptized?

I baptize you with water.
—Mark 1:8

John the Baptist is known for preparing the way for the ministry of Jesus Christ. He is also known for his baptismal services: "And so John came, baptizing in the desert region and preaching a baptism of repentance for the forgiveness of sins. The whole Judean countryside and all the people of Jerusalem went out to him. Confessing their sins, they were baptized by him in the Jordan River" (Mark 1:4-5).

Your baptism may be in a rustic outdoor venue such as a river or in a resplendent church setting. It's not the place that matters, but the attitude of your heart. Many congregations still perform baptisms outdoors, in private or public lakes, swimming pools, cattle watering tanks, even the ocean. Outdoor baptismal services have a unique and sacred beauty.

Yet indoor baptisms can be just as memorable. Many church buildings have built-in baptismal fonts or pools. Usually built into the platform area, they provide a convenient setting for the baptismal service. The pool is, most often, hidden from view by woodwork or decorations so that it blends in with the overall church decor. The modern baptismal pool has its own water and drainage system. Most are also heated for the comfort of the baptismal candidates. Steps, usually with an accompanying handrail, lead down into the waist-deep water of the pool. Certainly, it is a more comfortable setting than that experienced by the candidates in John the Baptist's time—but your baptism will be meaningful no matter what the setting.

- How important is the setting for your baptism?
- Have you spoken with your pastor about the setting?
- What is required to make baptism meaningful?

When Should I be Baptized?

*Paul said, "John's baptism was a baptism of repentance.
He told the people to believe in the one coming
after him, that is, in Jesus." On hearing this, they were
baptized into the name of the Lord Jesus.
—Acts 19:4-5*

Talk to your minister right away about your desire to be baptized. He or she has probably been eager to hear of this step of faith in your life. If others have expressed a desire for baptism, your pastor may already be planning a service, so don't hesitate to communicate with your minister about your desire to take part in a service of baptism. If you have health issues that would make it difficult or unwise for you to participate

in baptism, discuss them
with your minister or doctor.
Appropriate provisions can usually be made so that people with health
issues can experience this sacrament.

Should I wait until I'm further in my faith? Don't put off your baptism!
Take the necessary steps *now.* Procrastination will rob you of both
opportunity and spiritual victory. The enemy of your faith will throw fiery
darts of doubt and confusion to prevent you from being baptized: "Your
enemy the devil prowls around like a roaring lion looking for someone to
devour. Resist him, standing firm in the faith" (1 Pet. 5:8–9).

- Are you ready to be baptized?

- When will you speak with your pastor about baptism?

- How might your spiritual life be affected by putting off
  your baptism?

GENCY

What if I'm Anxious?

And the peace of God, which transcends all understanding,
will guard your hearts and your minds in Christ Jesus.
—Philippians 4:7

Some baptismal candidates have a fear of water. That is perfectly okay! It can be comforting to know that baptism takes only a matter of seconds from the moment the candidate enters the baptismal pool until he or she exits. The minister will make every effort to help you relax and feel comfortable so that you can focus on your baptism's meaning and significance.

Other candidates are concerned about their personal appearance during and after baptism, such as being seen with wet hair or wet clothing. Again, this is a very normal concern. Most congregations already have measures in place to provide for the modesty and comfort of baptismal candidates, such as private dressing and grooming areas. Ask your pastor what kind of accommodations you can expect.

Physical infirmities are another common area of concern to some candidates. Your minister will be glad to discuss any unusual circumstances

with you and assist in finding ways to make necessary adjustments or in identifying people who can provide physical assistance. Baptism can be conducted with great dignity for people with physical disabilities. Those who observe such services often comment on the beautiful display of personal sacrifice and discipline in allegiance to the Lord.

- What makes you anxious as you look ahead to your baptism?

- What special considerations might you need to discuss with your pastor?

- How might you experience the peace that transcends all understanding at your baptism?

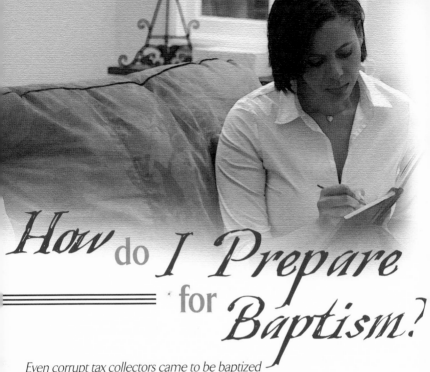

How do I Prepare for Baptism?

*Even corrupt tax collectors came to be baptized
and asked, "Teacher, what should we do?"*
—Luke 3:12, NLT

Prior to your baptism, your minister will provide instructions. Be sure to ask any questions you have and take time to acquaint yourself with the facilities. Try to picture in your mind how you will enter and exit the baptismal pool.

PREPAI

What should I wear? Some churches provide special baptismal clothing for candidates. Others simply instruct candidates to wear casual clothing that will not be damaged by the water. Avoid heavy sweaters, clothing that will cling to the body, or articles that will prevent you from changing in a speedy manner. A mental picture of your baptism will help you to select clothing that will be both functional and modest.

What will I be asked to do? Use the moments immediately prior to your baptism to reflect on what the Lord Jesus Christ has done for you—and in you. Make it a very special time of preparation and not one of meaningless chatter or cracking jokes.

When it is your turn, the minister will lead you into position. (Specific instructions are usually given both before and during the ceremony.) You may be asked for a verbal response, such as confession of Christ as Savior. The minister will then say a few words such as, "[Your name], I baptize you in the name of the Father, and of the Son, and of the Holy Spirit," and then you will be immersed and brought back up quickly.

What happens after baptism? You can probably head to the dressing room immediately. Remember to bring a complete change of clothing, a towel, and a plastic bag (for your wet clothes). Your minister will advise you further.

- What preparations do you need to make for your baptism?

- How will you use your time prior to your baptism?

- How might you identify with the Lord Jesus Christ by your baptism?

Step Into the Water and be Baptized

The sacrament of baptism is not itself salvation, but rather an outward sign of new life, the gift of God, budding in your heart. Baptism is a symbol that shows the entire world you have received Jesus Christ as the Lord of your life and it is your purpose to obey Him always.

That your testimony and your understanding of the significance of this holy act may be known, answer the following questions:

Do you believe in God the Father, the Son, and the Holy Spirit?